To

_____

From

_____

Living Christmas

EVERY DAY

HELEN STEINER RICE

Living Christmas

EVERY DAY

BARBOUR

A HELEN STEINER RICE® Product

© 2007 by the Helen Steiner Rice Foundation

All poems © Helen Steiner Rice Foundation Fund, LLC, a wholly owned subsidiary of Cincinnati Museum Center. All rights reserved.
Published under license from the Helen Steiner Rice Foundation Fund, LLC.

ISBN 978-1-61626-385-0

Devotional writing provided by Rebecca Currington in association with Snapdragon Group℠ Editorial Services.

Cover and interior illustrations: Greg Jackson, Thinkpen Design

Published by Barbour Publishing, Inc., P.O. Box 719, Uhrichsville, Ohio 44683, www.barbourbooks.com

Our mission is to publish and distribute inspirational products offering exceptional value and biblical encouragement to the masses.

Member of the
Evangelical Christian
Publishers Association

Printed in China.

CONTENTS

GIVING

PRAYER

THE GREATEST GIFT

Introduction

For one small window of time each year, the world around us shows its good side. Miracles of kindness and generosity abound, families gather and eat dinner together, neighbors pass cookies from door to door, and there are even stories of enemies laying down their weapons and sharing a meager meal on that one special day we call Christmas.

Have you ever wondered what it would be like to live in the world of Christmas all year long?

Though there are physical signs of Christmas all around us—trees, gifts, lights, decorations—the magic of the season is really not in things but in the thoughts and attitudes of the heart. We begin to ask what we can do for others rather than what we can do for ourselves. We humble ourselves before the image of a tiny child born to bring us eternal hope and peace and goodwill. And we celebrate love—God's love that gives and gives and keeps on giving!

As you read through the pages of this book, ask yourself if you are willing to make each day Christmas in your life. Let the outer trappings fall away, but allow the principal attributes of Christmas—selflessness, humility, hope, love, generosity, and kindness—to remain. The joyful, peaceful, and abundant heart is the one that celebrates Christmas every day.

Let Us Live
Christmas Every Day

Christmas is more than a day
at the end of the year,
More than a season
of joy and good cheer,

Christmas is really
God's pattern for living
To be followed all year
by unselfish giving. . .

For the holiday season
awakens good cheer
And draws us closer
to those we hold dear,

And we open our hearts
and find it is good
To live among men
as we always should. . .

But as soon as the tinsel
is stripped from the tree
The spirit of Christmas
fades silently

Into the background
of daily routine
And is lost in the whirl
of life's busy scene,

And all unawares
we miss and forgo
The greatest blessing
that mankind can know. . .

For if we lived Christmas
each day, as we should,
And made it our aim
to always do good,

We'd find the lost key
to meaningful living
That comes not from getting
but from unselfish giving. . .

And we'd know the great joy
of peace upon earth
Which was the real purpose
of our Savior's birth.

For in the glad tidings
of the first Christmas night
God showed us the way
and the truth and the light!

~ H S R

Celebration

Christmas and the Christ Child

In our Christmas celebrations
of merriment and mirth,
Let us not forget the miracle of
the holy Christ child's birth.
For in our festivities
it is easy to lose sight
Of the baby in the manger
and that holy, silent night.

~ H S R

God's Perfect Gift

Put your hope in the LORD, for with the LORD
is unfailing love and with him is full redemption.

PSALM 130:7 NIV

Every year it's the same; we rush around getting ready, preparing for one day when all our hopes and dreams will be realized. What did you wish for this year, dear friend? What special gift were you hoping to find under the tree? Was it there?

Once the gifts are unwrapped and the family has dispersed, many people feel disillusioned and depressed. Even when they've received what they thought they wanted, the good feeling rarely lingers. No earthly gift can really change your life—only God's gift can do that.

When God gave His Son, wrapped Him in flesh and laid Him in a humble manger, He gave us the hope of eternal life and much more. Along with Jesus came a bright future in God's holy presence and the promise of love and peace that will never end. Now that's a gift with staying power, a gift that will never disappoint or leave us feeling empty.

Christmas truly is a day to be celebrated—a day when we should break forth in song like the angel who announced Christ's birth—a day when we should feel joyful and excited and expectant—a day we should prepare for with great enthusiasm. But it should not be in anticipation of what we have yet to receive. Rather it should be in appreciation for what we have already been given—God's perfect gift, a Redeemer whose name is Jesus Christ.

Christmas Glitter

With our eyes
we see the glitter
of Christmas,
with our ears
we hear the merriment,
with our hands
we touch the
tinsel-tied trinkets,
but only
with our hearts
can we feel
the miracle of it.

~ H S R

Deck the Halls

*I will greatly rejoice in the LORD, my soul shall
be joyful in my God; for he hath clothed me with
the garments of salvation, he hath covered
me with the robe of righteousness.*

ISAIAH 61:10 KJV

Decorating for Christmas can be great fun, choosing the perfect tree and covering it with precious ornaments filled with memories of Christmases past. Some people love it so much that they light every corner and spend days hanging lights from the eaves of the house. A colorful wreath adorns the door and a beautiful centerpiece graces the Christmas dinner table.

Once the big decorating jobs are complete, the smaller ones begin. Each gift is wrapped in colorful paper, topped with beautiful bows, and placed with great care under the tree. For a time, each home is transformed into a magical wonderland of Christmas cheer. Many decorate right after Thanksgiving and keep their homes in splendor until the ringing in of the new year. Are you one of those people, dear friend?

Go all-out this Christmas. Deck the halls with boughs of holly, cover the tree with fabulous ornaments, dress each room in glitter. But don't let it distract you from the true miracle of what transpired on that holy day. Make sure the eyes of your heart are open to see beneath the glitter to the transforming Christ. Celebrate Christmas in your heart and when it's time for the physical decorations to come down, you'll continue to rejoice. Your heart will be full of God and His love throughout the cold winter months, the wet unpredictable spring, the waves of summer heat, and autumn's grandeur. Christmas will be with you all year long.

God Is Everywhere

Our Father up in heaven,
long, long years ago,
Looked down in His great mercy
upon the earth below

And saw that folks were lonely
and lost in deep despair.
And so He said, "I'll send My Son
to walk among them there,

So they can hear Him speaking
and feel His nearness, too,
And see the many miracles
that faith alone can do.

For if man really sees Him
and can touch His healing hand,
I know it will be easier
to believe and understand."

And so the holy Christ child
came down to live on earth.
And that is why we celebrate
His holy, wondrous birth,

And that is why at Christmas
the world becomes aware
That heaven may seem far away
but God is everywhere.

~ H S R

God's Eternal Flame

"I have loved you with an everlasting love."

JEREMIAH 31:3 NIV

Christmas is essentially the celebration of a miracle—God's only Son leaving the comfort and privilege of heaven's throne room and taking the form of a tiny human baby. In that one transaction, made in a borrowed manger among lowly animals, God gave all and man gained everything. Humanity, lost and broken, once again had hope. It has been more than two thousand years since that miracle took place, and yet it burns brighter than ever. It is an eternal flame.

Perhaps you have visited the grave of one of our nation's best-loved presidents—John F. Kennedy—and seen the gas-fed torch that burns there. Jacqueline Kennedy called it an "eternal flame," intended to celebrate his life and commemorate his death. Despite this designation, the torch has not burned constantly throughout the years. Repairs to the site and certain other conditions have extinguished the flame from time to time. And one day it, like every other mortal thing, will be snuffed out completely.

God's love, however, truly *is* an eternal flame. This flame, demonstrated by God's benevolent act of generosity and reconciliation, continues to burn brightly today. Though the powers of darkness, sin, and doubt have waged war against it, the flame is resilient. It burns in the hearts of all those who have lifted up their hands to God and received abundant love and forgiveness. Each day it spreads to new hearts and grows stronger still.

Christmas every day, dear friend, begins when your heart is set afire with the eternal flame of God's love—a flame ignited when Jesus Christ, God's Son, drew His first human breath. Without it Christmas is nothing more than glitter and empty promises. Does His flame burn faithfully in your heart?

Holly Wreaths

When holly wreaths are hanging
    upon each friendly door
And candles glow from windows
    and trees are trimmed once more,
It's pleasant to be sending
    this special wish to you
For all the season's happiness
    in everything you do.

           ~ H S R

The Prince of Peace

[Jesus said,] Behold, the kingdom of God is within you.

LUKE 17:21 KJV

One of God's greatest gifts to us, especially at Christmastime, is the gift of others. Family, friends, coworkers, neighbors, fellow believers, even strangers come together in a special way for the holidays. Bikers collect toys and deliver them to charities for distribution. Enthusiastic groups visit hospitals, nursing homes, and the homebound to hand out gifts to the sick and elderly. Mail carriers are loaded down with greetings from one family to another. It's like no other time of the year.

What do you imagine would happen if these things were commonplace all year? The homeless would never feel alone and alienated by their unfortunate circumstances. The elderly would cease to feel that they no longer have a purpose in this world. Disputes between neighbors would be offset by kind deeds and words of appreciation. Families would come together more often to express their love and devotion to one another. Dear friend, isn't that what life *should* be like?

This type of world is what God had in mind from the beginning. He always meant for us to live together in peace, for love to reign in our hearts and relationships, for goodwill to mark all our interactions.

When that tiny baby was born in Bethlehem, He was designated the Prince of Peace because He would bring to our hearts what was so badly needed in the world. Like a promise of good things to come, it would keep us looking for the day when all things are set right and we live in peace in the kingdom of God.

Let Us Keep Christ in Christmas

Christmas is a season for joy and merrymaking,
A time for gifts and presents—for giving and for taking,
A festive, friendly, happy time when everyone is gay,
And cheer, goodwill, and laughter are part of Christmas Day.
For God wants us to be happy on the birthday of His Son,
And that is why this season is such a joyous one,
For long ago the angels rejoiced at Bethlehem,
And down through the ages we have followed after them.

But in our celebrations of merriment and mirth,
Let us not forget the miracle of the holy Christ child's birth,
For in our gay festivities it's so easy to lose sight
Of the baby in the manger on that holy, silent night,
For Christmas in this modern world is a very different scene
From the stable and the Christ child so peaceful and serene,
And we often miss the mighty meaning and lose the greater glory
Of the holy little Christ child and the blessed Christmas story

If we don't keep Christ in Christmas and make His love a part
Of all the joy and happiness that fill our home and heart.
For without the holy Christ child, what is Christmas but a day
That is filled with empty pleasures that will only pass away.
But by keeping Christ in Christmas we are helping to fulfill
The glad tidings of the angels: peace on earth to men, goodwill.
And the Father up in heaven looking down on earth will say,
"You have kept Christ in your Christmas, now I'll keep you all the way."

~ H S R

The Heavenly Chorus

"He has raised up a horn of salvation for us in the house of his servant David. . .to rescue us from the hand of our enemies, and to enable us to serve him without fear in holiness and righteousness before him all our days."

LUKE 1:69, 74–75 NIV

Can you imagine, dear friend, what it must have been like for those lowly shepherds? Solitary by nature and comfortable with the quiet of the night, they must have been terribly shaken by the appearance of the angel of the Lord—not at some great distance but directly over their heads in their own fields. And the shepherds were not simply listening in as the angel spoke to some important ruler or dignitary. He was speaking directly to them! No wonder the angel's first words were "Be not afraid."

To their credit, the shepherds did not run but stood their ground, listening to all the angel had to tell them. And quite a story it was, followed by a musical presentation more spectacular than any the world has ever known. The shepherds took it all in—and then they acted on what they had heard. They went in search of the Christ child.

Unless we are prepared to lay our fears aside, hear the real message of Christmas, and act on what we have heard, it will be to us nothing more than a hollow celebration. Don't run from the child of Bethlehem, dear friend; run instead to His side. Take Him into your heart and your life. Make Him the center of your Christmas celebration and the reason for your life each day.

It's reasonable to assume that those shepherds were never the same after that night. It was likely the topic of conversation out in the fields from then on. It was also no doubt an experience that stayed with them when they were alone, the crowning event of each of their lives. When you meet the Christ child, your life will be changed as well—not for a day, but for eternity.

A Season of Kindness

May the kindly spirit of Christmas
　　spread its radiance far and wide,
So all the world may feel the glow
　　of this holy Christmastide.
Then may every heart and home continue
　　through the year
To feel the warmth and wonder
　　of this season of good cheer.
And may it bring us closer
　　to God and to each other
Till every stranger is a friend
　　and every man a brother.

~ H S R

Closer to God

"I am not alone because the Father is with me."

JOHN 16:32 NRSV

It could be that you find yourself alone this Christmas for any number of reasons. Perhaps you live far from family, or you've moved to a new place. Maybe you are one of many who does not have family. The season may seem sad because you've recently lost someone very dear to you. Or you may have experienced a financial setback or a health emergency, the ramifications of which have settled over the season like a wet blanket. When these things happen, the trappings of Christmas—lively Christmas music, happy shoppers in the mall, decorations everywhere you look—can send you tumbling into depression. Don't let your discouragement rob you of the happiest time of the year, dear friend. Turn your heart to God.

Though there may not be gifts to go under the tree, God has given you many gifts, the greatest of which is the gift of His Son, Jesus. In that straw-filled manger lay a child who represents all the promises of God—not just for others, but also for you personally. Those promises include a bright future, God's presence dwelling within you, eternal life and a heavenly home, peace that passes understanding, comfort in your grief, and love and joy unspeakable.

If you are alone this Christmas, sit down with your Bible and unwrap the gifts God has left for you there. Receive His peace, His love, His joy. And give Him what He wants most from you—your love in return. It will be a Christmas you will never forget. The best Christmas ever. The Christmas when you became part of God's family.

Too Nice to Forget

I wonder if you know the real reason
I send you a card every year at this season.
Do you think it's a habit I just can't break
Or something I do just for custom's sake?
I think I should tell you it's something more,
For to me Christmas opens the friendship door,
And I find myself reaching across the year
And clasping the hand of somebody dear.
To me it's a link I wouldn't want broken
That holds us together when words are unspoken,
For often through the year we have to forgo
Exchanging good wishes with those we know.
But Christmas opens the door of the heart,
And whether we're close or far apart,
When I write your name, I think of you
And pause to reflect and always renew
The bond that exists since we first met
And I found you somebody too nice to forget.

~ H S R

Heartfelt Greetings

Whatever you do, in word or deed,
do everything in the name of the Lord Jesus,
giving thanks to God the Father through him.

COLOSSIANS 3:17 NRSV

Do you send Christmas cards each year? More and more the custom of sending greetings during the holidays is falling away, due to lack of time, the expense of postage, and an unwillingness to add one more item to a long list of obligations.

Originally, the custom was intended to send greetings and news to friends and family to let them know they were loved and remembered.

Forget about sending cards to fulfill some misguided social obligation. Life is too short and Christmas is too precious to fill it with mindless activities just to impress others.

Forget about sending cards with nothing more than a store-bought greeting and an imprinted signature. This communicates only that the recipient was on your list. Nothing more.

Forget about sending cards to everyone you know—life is too short.

This year direct your effort in a more meaningful way by using this Christmas tradition to touch the lives of others. Add a personal note, even if it consists of just a few words. Something from the heart.

Sending cards at Christmas is a valuable opportunity to say the things you have been thinking all year. "I'm praying for you." "You aren't forgotten."

Jesus Christ was God's Christmas card to us. He told us that God still cared, that His love for us was still strong, that He hadn't forgotten us in our sinful state. His message was heartfelt and full of meaning. When you send your Christmas greetings this year, keep His example in mind.

In the Beauty
of a Snowflake

In the beauty of a snowflake,
Falling softly on the land,
Is the mystery and the miracle
Of God's great, creative hand.

~ H S R

Winter Wonderland

Since the creation of the world [God's]
invisible attributes are clearly seen, being
understood by the things that are made,
even His eternal power and Godhead.

ROMANS 1:20 NKJV

With all the activities of Christmas—decorating, shopping, parties, cards, church functions, to name just a few—it would seem there is precious little time to enjoy the natural beauty of the season. At any other time of the year, newly fallen snow might seem like a dreary, cold, isolating inconvenience. But at Christmas, it sparkles beneath the Christmas lights and crunches merrily under our feet. The night sky seems bright and mysterious as we consider the journey of the Magi and the shepherds in search of the Christ child. The air seems thick with excitement and possibilities.

God has given us so much to cherish, so much to remind us of His love and concern. And at Christmastime those things seem pronounced, enhanced by the natural beauty of God's creative hand.

During the holidays, stop long enough to notice God's natural world around you. Let the beauty of His creation add to your happiness and goodwill. Thank Him for the snowflakes that fall, the stars that twinkle overhead, and the air that we all take so much for granted. Thank Him, too, for hope and happiness and the possibility of even better things to come.

God is good—at Christmastime and every time. He has surrounded us with natural beauty and wonder. Let Him know how much you appreciate it.

Joy

Glory to God in the Highest

"Glory to God in the highest
and peace on earth to men"—
May the Christmas song the angels sang
stir in our hearts again
And bring a new awareness
that the fate of every nation
Is sealed securely in the hand
of the Maker of creation.
For man, with all his knowledge,
his inventions, and his skill,
Can never go an inch beyond
the holy Father's will,
For greater than the scope of man
and far beyond all seeing
In Him who made the universe,
man lives and has his being.

~ H S R

Behold the King!

[The angel said to Mary,] "You will name him Jesus. He will be great, and will be called the Son of the Most High, and the Lord God will give to him the throne of his ancestor David. He will reign over the house of Jacob forever, and of his kingdom there will be no end."

Luke 1:31–33 NRSV

Christmas seems like a personal holiday, doesn't it? Family gathered around. Rejoicing both in the heart and in the home. What we often forget is that Christmas holds great significance on a much larger scale. The far-reaching ramifications of that glorious event we all celebrate will one day rock the nations of the earth.

Jesus Christ was born with one goal in mind—that He might die! And His sacrifice changed everything. With it, He redeemed His creation—all of it. He paid the ransom for our souls, reclaimed His marvelous earth, and set in place an unalterable destiny for the nations of the world. He reestablished His authority as judge of all.

At Christmas, we should rejoice not only in the child lying in a manger-bed but also in the King of kings and

Lord of lords, the ruler of heaven and earth, for they are one and the same—His name is Jesus!

To leave Christ in the manger is to forget why He came in the first place. The celebration that surrounded His birth was simply a precursor to what was yet to come—the sacrifice, the miracle of the resurrection, the power and the glory of His heavenly kingdom.

Does Christ reign and rule in your life, dear friend? Do you know Him as both humble child and mighty King? When you offer Him your gifts this Christmas, bring them not to the manger, but lay them at the foot of His throne. Let the risen Christ take His place of honor in your heart and bring everlasting joy to your life at Christmas and all year.

This Is the Savior
of the World

Some regard the Christmas story as something beautiful to hear,
A lovely Christmas custom that we celebrate each year.
But it's more than just a story told to make our hearts rejoice;
It's our Father up in heaven speaking through
*   the Christ child's voice,*
Telling us of heavenly kingdoms that He has prepared above
For those who put their trust in His mercy and His love.
And only through the Christ child can man be born again,
For God sent the baby Jesus as the Savior of all men.

~ H S R

Heavenly Kingdoms

Unto [God] that is able to do exceeding abundantly above all that we ask or think, according to the power that worketh in us, unto him be glory in the church by Christ Jesus throughout all ages, world without end. Amen.

EPHESIANS 3:20–21 KJV

When you look out over a valley lush with wildflowers and all manner of vegetation, you might think there is nothing lovelier in all the world. Standing on the edge of the Grand Canyon and looking down on the magnificent splendor of God's earthly creation, you might ask yourself if anything can compare with its timeless beauty. The fragile petals of an orchid, the joyful rainbow that follows a gentle rain—they're more than our finite minds can contain.

So now, dear friend, consider this: The grandeur of this world is only a down payment on the riches that await us in heaven. Were it not for our resurrected bodies and redeemed minds, we would find heaven too overwhelming, too much to take in.

This Christmas as you meditate on the Christ child, remember that the gifts we have received from God are only the beginning. One day we will see the world as God intended it before sin dimmed its brilliance. We will look around us on that day and know that what we knew before was little more than a shadow of what was to come. In that day our joy will be complete.

This Christmas take some time to sit back, put your feet up, and imagine the wonders that lie ahead. Put your creative mind to the test, because no matter how grandiose your conception, it will fall short of the real thing.

Thank your heavenly Father for the gifts God will give in our future. Thank Him for the babe of Bethlehem who brought us more than we could ever ask or think.

Silent Night, Holy Night

Let us listen in silence so we may hear
The Christmas message more clearly this year.
Silently the green leaves grow,
In silence falls the soft, white snow,
Silently the flowers bloom,
In silence sunshine fills a room,
Silently bright stars appear,
In silence velvet night draws near,
And silently God enters in
To free a troubled heart from sin.
For God works silently in lives,
And nothing spiritual survives
Amid the din of a noisy street
Where raucous crowds with hurrying feet
And blinded eyes and deafened ears
Are never privileged to hear
The message God wants to impart
To every troubled, weary heart.
So let not our worldly celebrations
Disturb our Christmas meditations,
For only in a quiet place
Can we behold God face-to-face.

~ H S R

The Sounds of Christmas

Love the LORD your God, listen to his voice,
and hold fast to him. For the LORD is your life.

DEUTERONOMY 30:20 NIV

If you've been out shopping this Christmas, you know how noisy this season can be. Christmas music blares from every speaker. A din of voices rises to meet it. Even outdoors, the sounds of traffic, ringing bells, people coming and going in a hurry, chattering on their cell phones, add to the mix. It's tough to remember where you are, let alone what you're doing and why you're doing it. It's even more difficult to hear those things wrapped in silence. That's why it's important to step away long enough to listen for God's voice in all your busyness.

Every year we hear again the message God speaks to us through the birth of Christ, and each year it takes on deeper meaning. But God wants to speak other things to your heart as well. He wants to infuse you with peace and joy, give you a vision of the abundant life He's planned for you, give you understanding concerning who you are in regard to Him. Those messages are so important that they can only be heard in the stillness of your private time with Him.

There is a time to be in the spin of things, giving yourself to the hustle and bustle of the holidays. There is a time to sing and dance and celebrate the unspeakable excellence of God's gift to us. There is a time to fill your head with the joy of it all. And there is a time to be quiet and hear the gentle words of your Savior—words that will resound in your heart and mind long after the Christmas music fades and the bells stop their ringing.

The Mystery of Christmas

The wonderment in a small child's eyes,
The ageless awe in the Christmas skies,
The nameless joy that fills the air,
The throngs that kneel in praise and prayer—
These are the things that make us know
That men may come and men may go,
But none will ever find a way
To banish Christ from Christmas Day,
For with each child there's born again
A mystery that baffles men.

~ H S R

Shrouded in Mystery

*I will meditate on the glorious splendor of
Your majesty, and on Your wondrous works.*

PSALM 145:5 NKJV

The wonders of science are amazing. Microbes and organisms too small for the human eye to see have been discovered, studied, manipulated, and put to work for the benefit of humankind. Many diseases once considered deadly have been eradicated completely or reduced to a mere whimper. Athletes play basketball and run marathons on artificial limbs. It is now commonplace to transplant organs, skin, and countless other things from one person to another. But there is one thing that medical science will never achieve: only God can place an eternal spirit into a human body.

How the mighty Creator of the universe came to be a tiny baby in a Bethlehem stable is now and will always be a mystery to humankind. The Bible has given us the broad brushstrokes of how this miracle occurred—the Holy Spirit overshadowed a virgin girl named Mary—but how this exactly happened is simply too great for our brains to comprehend. But we don't understand other parts of God's plan, either. How were the oceans formed, when were the planets tossed into space, how do birds find their way back to their nests each year after a long journey south?

The birth of Christ is more than just the stellar moment in human history; it also is the most compelling reason possible to stand in awe of our great heavenly Father, to kneel before Him in praise and adoration, to let the joy inherent in His presence dwell within us.

Every child knows instinctively that Christ's birth is a wondrous miracle—and a mystery. Let your heart be filled with wonder as well.

The Miracle of Christmas

Miracles are marvels
That defy all explanation
And Christmas is a miracle
And not just a celebration—
For when the true significance
Of this so-called Christmas story
Penetrates the minds of men
And transforms them with its glory,
Then only can rebellious man,
So hate-torn with dissension,
Behold his adversaries
With a broader new dimension—
For we can only live in peace
When we learn to love each other
And accept all human beings
With the compassion of a brother—
And it takes the Christ of Christmas
To change man's point of view,
For only through the Christ child
Can all men be born anew. . .
And in the Christmas story
Of the holy Christ child's birth
Is the answer to a better world
And goodwill and peace on earth.

~ H S R

Prince of Peace

A child has been born for us, a son given to us;
authority rests upon his shoulders, and he is named
Wonderful Counselor, Mighty God,
Everlasting Father, Prince of Peace.

The Christ child was born into a violent world filled with conflict and discord. The emperor Herod, sensing that the child could be the fulfillment of the Messianic prophecy, had all the baby boys, two years of age and younger, born in the vicinity of Bethlehem slaughtered. Not even the children were safe from the brutality of those days. Jesus, a ruler designated the Prince of Peace, was truly an anomaly in those barbarous times. No wonder His disciples assumed His intention was to physically overthrow the wicked government and initiate a reign of peace.

The day the disciples hoped for will come one day. Jesus Christ will reign and rule on this earth. But His first coming was not to exert power over nations but rather to bring peace to human hearts.

Our world today is still filled with violence. Wars abound. Innocent blood is spilled on every continent, even our own. And our puny efforts at peace never bring lasting results—despite the selfless sacrifice of those who fight for it. But just as in Christ's day, we can choose to become His temple, to let peace reign within our own hearts and lives. We can choose love over hate, peace over discord, grace over judgment, caring over callousness, joy over sorrow. Until the day when we can physically dwell in God's kingdom, His kingdom can dwell in us! What a marvelous thing that is!

Open your heart to the Christ child. Though He no longer takes the form of a tiny infant, He is still accessible to the heart that seeks Him. Let His indwelling Spirit bring you peace, dear friend.

The Christmas Tree

Listen—be quiet—perhaps you can hear
The Christmas tree speaking, soft and clear:
I am God's messenger of love, and in my Christmas dress,
I come to light your heart and home with joy and happiness.
I bring you pretty packages and longed-for gifts of love,
But most of all I bring you a message from above—
The message Christmas angels sang on that first Christmas night
When Jesus Christ, the Father's Son, became this dark
    world's light.
For though I'm tinsel-laden and beautiful to see,
Remember, I am much, much more than just a glittering tree,
More than a decoration to enhance the Christmas scene,
I am a living symbol that God's love is evergreen,
And when Christmas Day is over and the holidays are through,
May the joyous spirit of Christmas abide all year with you.
So have a merry Christmas in the blessed Savior's name
And thank Him for the priceless gifts that are ours
    because He came.

                                                    ~ H S R

Oh Christmas Tree!

*[Jesus said,] "Seek the kingdom of God,
and all these things shall be added to you."*

LUKE 12:31 NKJV

There are many traditions associated with the Christmas tree. One has it that St. Boniface, instrumental in converting the German people to the Christian faith, came across a group of pagans worshipping an oak tree. Enraged, he cut down the tree. In its place a young fir tree sprang up from the roots of the old oak. Boniface saw this as a sign that as pagan worship was eradicated, Christian worship would rise up in its place.

We will never know if this tale is true, but we do know that across Europe, people used the tree to weave tales intended to teach their children about the celebration of Christ's birth. Martin Luther may have given the Christmas tree tradition its strongest advocacy. The story goes that he was out walking on a bright, snow-covered, starlit night pondering the birth of Christ. Enthralled by the evergreen trees, the stars, and the landscape, he took a tree inside and put candles on it to try to recapture the majesty he had experienced on his walk.

This year, make your Christmas tree a symbol of more than a well-decorated home. As you place the ornaments on its branches, let it remind you of the wonder of one magnificent night that changed everyone and everything forever. The angels sang. The star shone overhead. The shepherds brought their simple gifts. The Savior of the world lay sleeping in a humble manger. As you bring your tree inside, think about bringing the kingdom of God into your heart. Let your tree speak to you and to all those who see it. Let it speak a message of hope, peace, love, and joy.

May You Feel the Quiet Beauty

May you feel the quiet beauty
of that holy, silent night
When God sent the little Christ child
to be this dark world's light.
May you know the peace He promised,
may you feel His presence near,
Not only just at Christmas,
but throughout a happy year.

~ H S R

The Fearless Virgin

[Mary] gave birth to her firstborn, a son. She
wrapped him in cloths and placed him in a manger,
because there was no guest room available for them.

LUKE 2:7 NIV

Mary was so young, just a teenager. It must have
taken a great deal of courage and even more faith
for her to let Joseph lift her onto a donkey and lead her
away from familiar surroundings—and this knowing she
was so close to giving birth. But she had seen the angel
and heard his message. She believed that whatever
might happen, her life and the life of her child were in
God's hands.

What do you suppose she was thinking, dear friend,
as she and Joseph moved quietly along the road, settled
into the donkey's rhythmic sway? Perhaps she was
wondering what her child would look like—after all, He
was God's Son, not Joseph's. She may have been asking
herself how she would find the strength, the wisdom,
the understanding to raise such a child.

How do you think she felt when they arrived in
Bethlehem and found no room at all in which to stay?

Perhaps she whispered a prayer: "Oh God, is there no fitting place for Your own holy child to be born?"

Do you have Mary's faith, dear friend? Are you confident that God's plan will be fulfilled for your life, even when all the doors seem to be closed to you? Let God's peace and joy rest on you this Christmas as you ponder these questions. Mary knew that God was able, and that truth sustained her throughout the journey. Put your faith in God, just as Mary did. It will keep your heart filled with Christmas the whole year long.

Greeting Friends

It's Christmas and time to greet you once more,
But what can I say that I've not said before
Except to repeat at this meaningful season
That I have a deeply significant reason
For sending this greeting to tell you today
How thankful I am that you passed my way.

~ H S R

What a Friend
We Have in Jesus

[Jesus said,] "I have called you friends."

JOHN 15:15 NKJV

An eccentric but compassionate Irishman named Joseph Scriven fell ill while living in Canada in 1855. When a friend came by to check on him, he found a handwritten poem lying on the nightstand. When asked, Scriven said that he had written it for his mother in Ireland. She was in ill health, and he did not have the strength or financial means to visit her. The poem, entitled "Pray without Ceasing," was passed from person to person, and in 1886 it fell into the hands of Charles Converse, who set it to music and renamed it "What a Friend We Have in Jesus."

Have you ever imagined, dear friend, that Jesus, the baby born of Mary and laid in a straw-filled manger, wants to be your friend? And yet it's true! The Bible says so, and many—like Joseph Scriven—bear witness to the joy, peace, and comfort afforded through a relationship with God's Son.

Scriven certainly needed a friend. His heart was broken when his fiancée accidentally drowned on the eve of their wedding. He traveled to Canada to begin again and try to recover from his sorrow. Some time later, he once again fell in love. But this time his beloved contracted pneumonia and died. Scriven could have been bitter toward God, blaming Him for the tragedies. Instead, he experienced the friendship of God—big enough to bear all his sins and sorrows.

This Christmas and in the year ahead, carry in your heart not only the image of the Christ child but also that of the risen Jesus. Treat Him as a friend, and you will know a friendship greater than any you could imagine.

Giving

Christmas Is a
Season for Giving

Christmas is a season for gifts of every kind,
All the glittering, pretty things that Christmas shoppers find—
Baubles, beads, and bangles of silver and of gold—
Anything and everything that can be bought or sold
Is given at this season to place beneath the tree.
For Christmas is a special time for giving lavishly,
But there's one rare and priceless gift that can't be sold or bought.
It's something poor or rich can give, for it's a loving thought—
And loving thoughts are blessings for which no one can pay,
And only loving hearts can give this priceless gift away.

~ H S R

Abundantly Blessed

[Jesus] said to them, "Watch out! Be on your guard
against all kinds of greed; life does not consist in
an abundance of his possessions."

LUKE 12:15 NIV

We live in a country of privilege. If you aren't sure of that—go Christmas shopping. Stores are full to overflowing with every type of merchandise. It won't take long for you to see at least one item that you didn't know existed. Ingenuity truly is America's middle name. And unlike most nations of the world, this bounty is not reserved only for society's upper crust. It's available and, in most cases, affordable for everyone.

Yes, we are blessed—very much so. That blessing may be the reason we often focus on the material things and overlook the far more important spiritual aspects of the season. We enter the holidays bedazzled and distracted by those things money can buy. Even those people who don't have much are often preoccupied with what they can't afford.

Setting things right may not mean avoiding the stores altogether or praying you will fall into poverty in order to know true riches. Just make it a matter of choice to focus on the priceless and refuse to be swept off your feet by the rest.

Your approach to the holidays is in your hands, dear friend. Shopping, giving, receiving—none of these are wrong, especially when they are done with a right spirit. But when you put Christ first in Christmas, every other aspect of the holidays will seem even more significant. You will realize how abundantly blessed you really are.

The Gift of God's Love

All over the world at this season,
Expectant hands reach to receive
Gifts that are lavishly fashioned,
The finest that man can conceive. . .
For purchased and given at Christmas
Are luxuries we long to possess,
Given as favors and tokens
To try in some way to express
That strange, indefinable feeling
Which is part of this glad time of year
When streets are crowded with shoppers
And the air resounds with good cheer. . .
But back of each tinsel-tied package
Exchanged at this gift-giving season,
Unrecognized often by many,
Lies a deeper, more meaningful reason. . .
For born in a manger at Christmas
As a gift from the Father above,
An infant whose name was called Jesus
Brought mankind the gift of God's love. . .
And the gifts that we give have no purpose
Unless God is part of the giving,
And unless we make Christmas a pattern
To be followed in everyday living.

~ H S R

The Gift of Jesus

*Fixing our eyes on Jesus, the pioneer and
perfecter of our faith. For the joy set before him he
endured the cross, scorning its shame, and sat down
at the right hand of the throne of God. Consider him
who endured such opposition from sinners,
so that you will not grow weary and lose heart.*

HEBREWS 12:2–3 NIV

Ask a child about Christmas and you are apt to hear
an enthusiastic list of items he or she is hoping to
receive. Ask a parent and you will probably hear a list of
complaints about the price of the must-have toy of the
year. It would seem that gift giving has become something of a free-for-all for kids and an exhausting labor
for adults. Even after the children are taken care of,
there are many challenges.

"What can we get Aunt Marge? She has everything."

"My sister is giving my mom and dad something
really expensive this year. I don't know how we can
match it."

"It's going to be next Christmas before we pay off all
these credit card charges."

Somewhere in all this gift-giving madness, the real, the rare, the priceless gift of Christmas gets lost.

Enjoy opening the gifts under the tree this year, but be sure that your family knows that the greatest gift of all cannot be bought or sold at any price, but it is available to the youngest child and the oldest adult. The Prince of Peace, whose birth is celebrated on Christmas morning, represents God's love, forgiveness, reconciliation, and adoption into His family. In light of that, we can think only of giving to others with hearts of humility and gratitude. This could mean giving Aunt Marge something you've never before considered—a gift of your time and your love.

A Gift of Joy

As once more we approach the birthday of our King,
Do we search our hearts for a gift we can bring?
Do we stand by in awe like the small drummer boy
Who had no rare jewels, not even a toy
To lay at Christ's crib like the wise men of old,
Who brought precious gifts of silver and gold?
But the drummer boy played for the infant child,
And the baby Jesus looked up and smiled,
For the boy had given the best he had,
And his gift from the heart made the Savior glad.
Today He still smiles on all those who bring
Their heart to lay at the feet of the King.

~ H S R

What Will You Give Jesus?

*My heart leaps for joy, and
with my song I praise him.*

PSALM 28:7 NIV

Are your gifts all purchased, wrapped, and carefully stacked under the tree? If so, you are probably one of those rare individuals who has been working all year to find just the right gift for each member of the family. No quick, impulsive choices for you. You've done your homework and found the perfect gift for each individual. But have you asked yourself, "What am I giving to Jesus this year?"

When the shepherds and wise men found their way to the manger to see the Christ child, they carried with them gifts. The shepherds of small means brought what they had—their songs, their hearts, their worship. Their gifts spoke of humility and sacrifice. They gave of their lack. The Magi, who probably found Jesus when He was about two years old, brought gifts fit for a king. Gold, frankincense, and myrrh. Their gifts were lavish and well thought-out: gold was a gift for a king;

frankincense was a priestly gift; and myrrh foretold of His death and resurrection.

When it comes to giving your best to Jesus, dear friend, you would be wise to follow the example of both the shepherds and the wise men. Give of your very best to those who cannot return your generosity. In so doing, you honor Jesus as a benevolent King who cares about the needs of the poor and suffering, a ruler worthy of our praise and admiration. Give your heart, your love, your self, and you are emulating the shepherds' gifts of gentleness and grace.

What will you give Jesus this year?

Give Lavishly!
Live Abundantly!

The more you give, the more you get;
The more you laugh, the less you fret;
The more you do unselfishly,
The more you live abundantly.

The more of everything you share,
The more you'll always have to spare.
The more you love, the more you'll find
That life is good and friends are kind.

For only what we give away
Enriches us from day to day.
So let's live Christmas through the year
And fill the world with love and cheer.

~ H S R

The Laws of God

[Jesus said,] "Give, and it will be given to you. A good measure, pressed down, shaken together and running over, will be poured into your lap. For with the measure you use, it will be measured to you."

LUKE 6:38 NIV

Have you ever heard of the Law of Reciprocity? Many call it a spiritual law. Simply stated, it says that when you give, you receive. Jesus laid it out clearly in the Beatitudes. "Blessed are the merciful, for they will be shown mercy" (Matthew 5:7 NIV). You've almost certainly seen it in action. Some people choose to identify it by saying, "What goes around comes around." It's true—for the most part, we tend to get back what we hand out.

Some might argue that this can't possibly be a law because laws are immutable—they work every time and there are times when you show kindness and get harshness in return, or you give friendship and receive betrayal, or you give love and receive hatred. That's why this principle is called a spiritual law. It is calculated by God. When you show mercy, are you always shown mercy in return? Not always. Nothing is certain when you're dealing with human beings. But you can be sure of this: when you show mercy, God notices. He sees and remembers and rewards in your time of need.

Christmas is a wonderful time to practice the Law of Reciprocity. There are so many opportunities to give unselfishly to others. Open your heart and let blessings flow. Show them love, caring, kindness, compassion. Sow laughter and enthusiasm into the lives of others. Give without hesitation and without measure. One day soon you will find that when you most need a friend, you will have one. When you most need a laugh, you will have one. When you most need mercy, it will be poured out on you. It's not just a good idea; it's a law.

The Season of Giving

Christmas is a season of giving,
And giving is the key to living.
So let us give ourselves away,
Not just at Christmas but every day.
And remember a kind and thoughtful deed,
Or a hand outstretched in time of need,
Is the rarest of gifts for it is a part
Not of the purse but a loving heart,
And he who gives of himself will find
True joy of heart and peace of mind.

~ H S R

Christmas in the Heart

*"I will put my law in their minds
and write it on their hearts. I will be
their God, and they will be my people."*

JEREMIAH 31:33 NIV

What does it mean to celebrate Christmas all year long? Are we talking about leaving the tree and decorations up until the holiday season comes around again? Of course not. It means saving the best of what you receive this year, holding it close, cherishing it. And relishing the best of what you've given away. It means keeping the best of Christmas tucked away in your heart, where it can influence your thoughts and your actions throughout the year.

As you remove the decorations from the tree this year, think about what makes those ornaments so special—precious memories of loved ones who are no longer with you, happy times spent with family, joy and thanksgiving for blessings received. Store the ornaments in a box to be placed on the shelf, but store the memories in your heart where you can touch them every day.

When it's time to drag the tree out to the curb or put it back in its box, remind yourself that its green branches symbolized God's never-ending love for you. Though the symbol perishes, God's love never will.

Now as you restore the rooms of your home to their usual post-holiday beauty, whisper a prayer of thanksgiving, dear friend, for all God has done for you and those you love.

One more thing: To remind yourself that Christmas is stored in your heart, choose one ornament to remain on display throughout the year—perhaps a nativity, an angel, or a star to remind you to continue giving to others and receiving from God throughout the coming year.

Heart Gifts

It's not the things that can be bought
    that are life's richest treasure,
It's just the little "heart gifts"
    that money cannot measure. . .
A cheerful smile, a friendly word,
    a sympathetic nod
Are priceless little treasures
    from the storehouse of our God. . .
They are the things that can't be bought
    with silver or with gold,
For thoughtfulness and kindness
    and love are never sold. . .
They are the priceless things in life
    for which no one can pay,
And the giver finds rich recompense
    in giving them away.

~ H S R

The Very Best Gift

*Each of you should give what you have decided in your
heart to give, not reluctantly or under compulsion,
for God loves a cheerful giver.*

2 CORINTHIANS 9:7 NIV

Of all the gifts you give this year, there is one that
will be appreciated more than any other. The
problem is that this gift is costly, maybe because it's
one of a kind. Most people would say that they simply
can't afford it. Others say they would rather give something else—something less personal.

If you can find the means, though, this gift always
steals the show. Everyone likes it. Everyone! It has been
known to provide great joy for some, comfort and relief
for others. It doesn't come from some machine, that's
for sure. It's adept at identifying and meeting needs.

What is this gift, you ask? It's the gift of yourself.
Your time, your attention, your effort, your thoughtfulness, your affection.

Maybe you've never thought of yourself as God's
gift to others. But if you haven't, you need to start, dear
friend. God created the world and all the creatures in

it. Then He reached up and placed it in the universe—which He also created. God has always been a giver. But it wasn't until He gave humankind the gift of Himself that we began to understand the exquisite nature of our Creator God.

Reach out this Christmas and follow in the footsteps of your Savior. Give some of your hugs to someone who lives alone. Give some of your smiles to someone who is having a bad day. Give some of your time to visit with the elderly.

Jesus Christ gave all of Himself for you. Can you give of yourself to others?

Prayer

O God, Our Help in Ages Past

"O God, our help in ages past,
Our hope in years to be"—
Look down upon this present
And see our need of Thee. . .
For in this age of unrest,
With danger all around,
We need Thy hand to lead us
To higher, safer ground. . .
We need Thy help and counsel
To make us more aware
That our safety and security
Lie solely in Thy care. . .
And so we pray this Christmas
To feel Thy presence near
And for Thy all-wise guidance
Throughout the coming year. . .

~ H S R

Prayer for the Nation

I urge, then, first of all, that petitions, prayers,
intercession and thanksgiving be made for all people—
for kings and all those in authority, that we may live
peaceful and quiet lives in all godliness and holiness.

1 TIMOTHY 2:1–2 NIV

Christmas is unique in that it celebrates an event
that changed both the world at large and indi-
vidual hearts of men and women. On the larger scale,
Jesus' birth turned the world around Him upside
down. Herod, in a panic to protect his power, sent his
men to murder all the infant baby boys in and around
Bethlehem. He mistakenly thought he could kill the
Messiah before He could become a threat. Fortunately,
Jesus was not killed by Herod's men. An angel warned
Joseph in a dream, and he took Mary and Jesus to safety.

Though the world of that time was unreceptive,
there were those who were praying—righteous men and
women like Simeon and Anna who presided over Jesus'
dedication. They were praying for God's deliverance,
for the appearance of the Messiah, for the redemption

of Israel. And God was listening. He heard and answered their prayers.

Our world today is in turmoil. Our nation is divided. God has been locked out of our schools and government institutions. We see violence and brutality all around us. Injustice is the rule rather than the exception. The world at large has rejected Jesus, but there are those who are praying.

There is no better time than the Christmas season to offer prayers to God on behalf of our nation. Commit yourself to a specific prayer time each day. Anna and Simeon were richly blessed for their faithfulness. They were allowed to hold the Christ child, knowing that He represented redemption for Israel. You will be blessed as well, dear friend.

God Bless You at Christmas

God bless you at Christmas
And go with you through the year,
And whenever you are troubled
May you feel His presence near.
May the greatness of His mercy
And the sweetness of His peace
Bring you everlasting comfort
And the joys that never cease.

~ H S R

Christmas All Year Long

*Whatever is true, whatever is noble, whatever
is right, whatever is pure, whatever is lovely,
whatever is admirable—if anything is excellent
or praiseworthy—think about such things.*

PHILIPPIANS 4:8 NIV

Many of us go through our lives almost as sleepwalkers. We take care of our responsibilities, do our jobs, have a little fun from time to time. But we fail to live in a life-changing awareness of our Christian faith. We fail to realize to a large extent the benefits of having God in our lives. We don't really comprehend the immensity of the gift we received when God sent His Son to earth.

The wonderful thing about Christmas, dear friend, is that for a little while, a few weeks in the winter each year, the ordinary changes to extraordinary. We see things with a different eye. We focus in on a humble family in a stable looking down at a baby in a wooden crèche, farm animals peacefully standing nearby. We remind ourselves that Jesus Christ was born and sacrificed His life in order to make us children and heirs of God Almighty.

This Christmas let's make it our prayer that we keep the Christ child ever near in our hearts and our minds throughout the year. Each day thank your heavenly Father for His love and faithfulness, and ask Him to show you yet another of His many benefits. Chances are you will have an excellent year, a year filled with excitement and discovery, a year filled with gratitude and thanksgiving. You will almost certainly find yourself loving more, giving more, laughing more, living more.

Leave your sleepwalking days behind and live each day celebrating God's glorious presence in your everyday life.

A Christmas Prayer

Oh Father up in heaven,
We have wandered far away
From the holy little Christ child
Who was born on Christmas Day.
And the peace on earth You promised,
We have been unmindful of,
Not believing we could find it
In a simple thing called love.
We've forgotten why You sent us
Jesus Christ, Your only Son,
And in arrogance and ignorance
It's our will, not Thine, be done.
Oh, forgive us, heavenly Father,
Teach us how to be more kind,
So that we may judge all people
With our heart and not our mind.
And, oh God, in Thy great goodness,
May our guidance Christmas night
Be the star the wise men followed—
Not a man-made satellite.

~ H S R

The Seat of the Forgiven

*"You are a God ready to forgive, gracious and merciful,
slow to anger and abounding in steadfast love."*

NEHEMIAH 9:17 NRSV

If you had to sum it up, how would you say you have
conducted your life this past year? Perhaps you've
tried to live well and still found yourself doing things
you aren't proud of. God isn't interested in why we sin.
He knows it is simply part of our nature. That's why it
was so important for Jesus—the sacrifice for our sins—
to be born possessing God's holiness and purity. The
virgin birth was not simply added to the story to give it
a unique touch. Jesus Christ was *all* God and *all* man. He
alone qualified as a ransom for our redemption.

The baby in Bethlehem's manger was the only hope
for a sin-scarred world. He was and is the only hope for
you as well. As Christmas approaches, take time out to
spend with your Savior. Lay all your failings at His feet.
He will heal your wounds and dispatch your misdeeds
into the ocean of forgetfulness. Then He will give you
a new life, one worthy of your calling as a child of the
most high God.

Forgiveness is a precious thing. One of Jesus' followers poured oil on His feet and wiped them with her hair. She knew what she had been given. She understood the gravity of it. She was overcome with gratitude.

Pray the prayer of repentance this Christmas and thank God for it. Just as with the woman who honored Jesus with her gift, God's love will lift you up, wash you clean, and set you in the seat of the forgiven.

A Christmas Prayer of Praise

Praise God, the Holy One,
For giving us His only Son
To live on earth as mortals do
To draw us closer, God, to You.
Praise the Father for all things
And for the message Christmas brings.
This is indeed the day of days
To raise your voice in prayers of praise—
For we would have nowhere to go
When life has ended here below,
For redemption came and salvation was won
Through Jesus Christ, the Father's Son.

~ H S R

Take the Hand of God

May your hand be ready to help me,
for I have chosen your precepts. I long for your
salvation, LORD, *and your law gives me delight.*

PSALM 119:173–174 NIV

The story of Christ's birth as recorded by both St.
Luke and St. Matthew raises one theme above
all—praise and worship. The shepherds and the Magi
praised the child, and the sky was aflame with angelic
worshippers. Even the universe praised His name as one
of the brightest stars in the firmament took flight and
settled over the simple stable where the Christ child
quietly slept.

It was a time of celebration. God's plan of redemption had left the planning stages and was in motion. The
antidote for sin finally had form and substance. Help
was on the way.

Christmas is truly Christmas, settled deep within
your heart, when you can look past the bustling crowds,
the planning, shopping, baking, and decorating, and
recognize the momentous nature of what occurred in
that quiet stable. Light quenched the darkness, despair

was replaced with hope, reconciliation became possible. In short, God extended His hand to us, to you.

Join in the chorus this Christmas. Sing along with the angels. Let words of praise fall from your lips as they did from the shepherds. Present Him with gifts as the Magi did—the gift of your heart. Praise Him, dear friend, for His kindness, for His mercy, for His love. Receive His offer of adoption. Rejoice in your new estate.

Praise is a prayer—a prayer of earnest devotion. Don't make another preparation until you have first praised Him from your heart.

A Christmas Prayer of Blessing

"Our Father, who art in heaven,"
hear this Christmas prayer,
And if it be Thy gracious will,
may joy be everywhere—

The joy that comes from knowing
that the holy Christ child came
To bless the earth at Christmas
for Thy sake and in Thy name.

And with this prayer there comes a wish,
that these holy, happy days
Will bless your loved ones everywhere
in many joyous ways.

~ H S R

You Are Blessed!

*Praise be to the God and Father of our Lord
Jesus Christ, who has blessed us in the heavenly
realms with every spiritual blessing in Christ.*

EPHESIANS 1:3 NIV

The journey had been long, hour after hour on the back of a donkey. No wonder by the time Joseph and Mary arrived in Bethlehem, she was ready to deliver. And then the news: no rooms were available—not one. This must have been a jarring blow for a woman in Mary's condition. Would she be asked to give birth in the city streets?

As inadequate as it was, the couple probably was relieved when a kind innkeeper allowed them to stay the night in his stable. At least there they would be off the streets and out of the elements. Mary gave birth there with none of the considerations typically afforded a mother in her condition—no experienced person to assist, no light, no heat, no comfortable bed, no recourse if something should go wrong.

Oddly, the account of the Nativity says nothing about Mary crying out in despair or Joseph sick with worry and anxiety. The two seem calm, gratefully and completely resigned to God's plan. They knew beyond a shadow of a doubt that this child was God's own. He would be watching, attending, caring for them. They realized what a blessing it was to be part of this incredible event. No difficulty or hardship could put a damper on that.

You also belong to God, dear friend, and as such you are blessed. No matter what difficulties you may face, quietly reflect on that truth. Let it transform your surroundings and overshadow your circumstances. You are blessed.

A Christmas Prayer
for Peace

We pray to Thee, our Father,
    as Christmas comes again,
For peace among all nations
    and goodwill among all men.
Give us strength and courage
    to search ourselves inside
And recognize our vanity,
    our selfishness and pride.
For the struggle of all ages
    is centered deep within
Where each man has a private war
    that his own soul must win.
For a world of peace and plenty,
    of which all men have dreamed,
Can only be attained and kept
    when the spirit is redeemed.

~ H S R

We All Want Peace

*Grace and peace to you from God our
Father and the Lord Jesus Christ.*

EPHESIANS 1:2 NIV

When people are given the choice, the virtue they choose is not happiness or even love—it's usually peace. We humans have fragile nervous systems; we long for relief from the shaking, jarring, wearing of stress and turmoil. We long for peace and calm. We long for it globally, nationally, and of course personally.

Why not make peace your prayer this Christmas? Make peace a priority. Are you struggling in your work life? Chasing success, stressing out over office politics, worrying that your job could be eliminated? Ask God for peace. What about your relationships? Are there problems with your parents, your children, your friends? Do family gatherings, like those so popular this time of year, give you a splitting headache? How are you doing personally? Are you stressed out, barely holding off an ulcer, never settled or satisfied with who you really are?

The scriptures call Jesus the Prince of Peace. They acknowledge that He was sent because of love—but what He came to bring us is peace. We also know that He accomplished His mission. So why do we have so little of what we need from Him? Perhaps it's because we are looking in all the wrong places. We are searching outside of ourselves, thinking that people, possessions, and other externals can bring us peace. Bethlehem's babe is the only source of real peace, and He is eager to give us what we need. Make peace a priority this year.

"I Am the Light of the World"

Oh Father, up in heaven,
*   we have wandered far away*
From the holy little Christ child
*   who was born on Christmas day,*
And the promise of salvation
*   that God promised when Christ died.*
We have often vaguely questioned,
*   even doubted and denied. . .*
We've forgotten why God sent us
*   Jesus Christ, His only Son,*
And in arrogance and ignorance
*   it's our will, not Thine, be done. . .*
Oh, forgive us our transgressions
*   and stir our souls within*

And make us ever conscious
    that there is no joy in sin
And shed Thy light upon us
    as Christmas comes again
So we may strive for peace on earth
    and goodwill among men. . .
And, God, in Thy great wisdom,
    Thy mercy, and Thy love,
Endow man with the virtue
    that we have so little of. . .
For unless we have humility
    in ourselves and in our nation,
We are vain and selfish puppets
    in a world of automation,
And with no God to follow
    but the false ones we create,
We become the heartless victims
    of a Godless nation's fate. . .
Oh, give us ears to hear Thee
    and give us eyes to see,
So we may once more seek Thee
    in true humility.

~ H S R

Worship Him!

Come, let us bow down in worship, let us kneel before the LORD our Maker; for he is our God and we are the people of his pasture, the flock under his care.

PSALM 95:6–7 NIV

Christmas is such a busy time of year. It doesn't really lend itself well to quiet reflection—but it should. You might imagine that Mary was reflecting as she watched over her infant Son lying in the manger. When the shepherds and the Magi paid their respects, the Bible doesn't mention that she said a word. Perhaps she did, but we just don't know. And it's certainly easy to understand why she would be silent. What is there to say about something so utterly remarkable, so unspeakably amazing?

If you wish this year to really celebrate the birth of Christ, you will need to see it as Mary did—more than a religious exercise or a fun-packed holiday, more than friends and family, gifts and decorations. You will have to focus more on the Person of Christmas than the taste of fudge and divinity. You will have to take time out to truly appreciate what God did for you on that cold winter morning, dear friend. When you do, you may be as speechless as Mary presumably was. But God doesn't mind. He welcomes your silent adoration, your time of quiet as you reflect on His love, His mercy, His faithfulness, His humility, His peace, His forgiveness.

Find a moment to slip away and simply be quiet before Him. Let your heart take charge rather than your head. Even though you speak no words, your actions amount to a prayer of love and adoration, of contrition and thankfulness. Give yourself to worship.

Keep Christ in Christmas

If we keep Christ in Christmas
He will keep us every day,
And when we are in His keeping
and we follow in His way,
All our little, earthly sorrows,
all our worries and our cares,
Seem lifted from our shoulders
when we go to God in prayer.

~ H S R

Comfort and Joy!

*Those the L*ORD* has rescued will return. . . .*
Gladness and joy will overtake them,
and sorrow and sighing will flee away.

ISAIAH 35:10 NIV

When Christmas is truly in our hearts, dear friend, it can't be confined to a particular day, or month, or season. It is ongoing, always new, always bright every morning. Christ has been born not only in a manger in Bethlehem but also in our hearts. He is there to bring us peace, joy, and love. He is there to help us bequeath goodwill to all those around us. He is there to constantly remind us that we have been given entrance into the throne room of Almighty God.

Take a small ornament from the tree this year as you pack the others away. Keep it close by—on the end table next to your bed, above your kitchen sink, on a shelf in your living room, on your desk at the office. When you feel worried or sad, let that little ornament speak to you, a visual reminder of who is living in your heart—the Light of the World, the Prince of Peace, your Redeemer. He will comfort you and guide you and help you in every aspect of your life. He doesn't care if it's January, June, or December. He is there for you—always!

As you find a good place for your ornament, whisper a prayer of thanksgiving to the One who was born to die for you. Ask Him to help you make Christmas more than a seasonal holiday. Ask Him to help you make it a time of great comfort and joy all year long.

Let Us Pray on This Holy Christmas Day

What better time and what better season,
What greater occasion or more wonderful reason
To kneel down in prayer and lift our hands high
To the God of creation, who made land and sky.
And, oh, what a privilege as the new year begins
To ask God to wipe out our errors and sins
And to know when we ask, if we are sincere,
He will wipe our slate clean as we start a new year.
So at this glad season when joy's everywhere,
Let us meet our Redeemer at the altar of prayer.

~ H S R

The Privilege of Prayer

*[The LORD says,] "It shall come to pass
that before they call, I will answer; and
while they are still speaking, I will hear."*

ISAIAH 65:24 NKJV

Prayer is a wonderful privilege, an honor that sets us apart. We alone have access to the throne room of God—not for purposes of judgment but because He has added us to His family, made us heirs to His kingdom. We have been invited in, dear friend. For us, there is no fear of faltering in our speech or fainting before Him. We can proceed with perfect confidence that we will be acknowledged, listened to, and cared for. For this reason, prayer is not a confrontation but a communication—simple interaction between Father and child.

Our adoption was not an easy one to arrange. There were issues like sin and rebellion and waywardness, but God was determined. So determined, in fact, that He built a bridge with His own body, born of a virgin, laid in a manger. Jesus Christ was born, betrayed, and crucified for our wrongdoing. But He did not remain in the grave. He was raised to newness of life and with His victory won us right standing with God the Father.

Our Christmas prayer should always be that we are thankful to be God's beloved children, standing before Him in the purity and holiness of Christ Himself. We should come as the shepherds and the Magi who, regardless of their social or material standing, all bowed their knees before Him in adoration. Won't you make this your prayer? Pray it as you shop, bake, wrap packages, sign cards, and decorate. "Dear Jesus, I adore You. I bow my heart before You."

The
Greatest
Gift

The Christmas Story

Christmas is more than a dramatized tradition—
It's God's promise to all men
That only through the Christ child
Can we be born again.
It's God's assurance of a future
Beyond all that we have dreamed,
For Jesus lived on earth and died
So that we might be redeemed.
Mankind's hope and salvation
Are in the Christmas story,
For in these words there are revealed
God's greatness and His glory.

~ H S R

Beyond the Manger

I kneel before the Father. . . . I pray that out of his glorious riches he may strengthen you with power through his Spirit in your inner being, so that Christ may dwell in your hearts through faith.

EPHESIANS 3:14–17 NIV

There are three kinds of people in this world. There are those who celebrate Christmas without ever considering that it is far more than a fable—the simple story of a mother and father stranded far from home. These people are like the innkeeper. They love to adore Him in the stable but have no room for Him in their own hearts and lives. Others have opened their hearts to the Christ, but they see Him only as a small child, holy but helpless. These people love God and are grateful for the gift of His Son, but they are unaware of everything the gift provides.

The third group consists of those who have invited Christ into their hearts and understand that in so doing they have become temples of the living God. They know with great assurance that the baby has grown and fulfilled His mission of redemption. They have become children of the King of kings. These people worship a mighty, living Christ rather than a baby in a manger— holy though He might be.

What kind of person are you? If you find that you are in one of the first two groups, you should know that there is so much more than you may have imagined. Rather than closing the office and going to bed for the night as the innkeeper did, journey through the night like the Magi, leave all else behind like the shepherds. Don't stop until you find the child, and then know Him for all He is—holy baby, suffering Savior, and risen Lord. When you have done this, you have truly experienced Christmas.

The First Christmas Morn

In this world of violence and hatred and greed
Where men lust for power and scorn those in need,
What could we hope for and where could we go
To find comfort and courage on this earth below
If in Bethlehem's manger Christ had not been born
Many centuries ago on the first Christmas morn?
For life everlasting and eternal glory
Were promised to man in the first Christmas story.

~ H S R

The Majesty of It All

All this is from God, who reconciled us to himself
through Christ and gave us the ministry of
reconciliation: that God was reconciling the world
to himself in Christ, not counting
people's sins against them.

2 CORINTHIANS 5:18–19 NIV

Christmas morning—the *first* Christmas morning—try to imagine it. Artists have painted the beautiful scene. Authors and poets have used words to describe the magical setting. Songwriters and musicians have celebrated its majesty. But wait! Weren't those real animals in that stable, real straw in the manger, real people huddled together in the cold? The shepherds were likely smelly, the Magi fatigued from their long journey—and Mary. . .she must have been exhausted and uncomfortable from her long and painful ordeal. That's the reality.

But isn't that how we all present ourselves to Jesus? Sin-stained, weary, burdened with cares, dusty and dirty from life. And just as the holy child received His worshippers, the risen Christ receives us. In the stable on the first Christmas morning, supernatural splendor eclipsed earthly reality. And on the day we bow our knee to our Lord, His perfection and righteousness eclipse our sin and waywardness. We are made acceptable.

Don't hesitate to worship the Christ because you feel somehow unworthy. He will receive you. He urges you to come as you are, to enter in, to bow down, to worship. He has done more than suspend reality; He has overruled it. He has created a new reality filled with hope and joy and reconciliation. The artists, the authors, the poets, the songwriters, and the musicians were right all along.

What if Jesus had chosen not to come to earth, not to be born as a baby, not to carry our sin on His shoulders? The reality is that He did, and that's a beautiful picture.

In Christ Who Was Born at Christmas All Men May Live Again

Let us all remember,
When our faith is running low,
Christ is more than just a figure
Wrapped in an ethereal glow—
For He came and dwelt among us
And He knows our every need
And He loves and understands us
And forgives each sinful deed—
He was crucified and buried
And rose again in glory,
And His promise of salvation
Makes the wondrous Christmas story
An abiding reassurance
That the little Christ child's birth
Was the beautiful beginning
Of God's plan for peace on earth.

~ H S R

God's Plan Restored

*"I have swept away your offenses like a
cloud, your sins like the morning mist.
Return to me, for I have redeemed you."*

ISAIAH 44:22 NIV

When God gave Adam and Eve free will, He must
have known it would go badly. After all, He
knows everything from beginning to end. He knew
exactly when they would turn out of the path He had
so masterfully set before them and sin would be intro-
duced into His perfect world. He knew. He could have
given up, written the project off. He might have said to
Himself that giving created beings free will was always a
losing proposition. They just couldn't be trusted.

But He didn't. Instead He made a plan—one that
would provide a way for sin to be forgiven rather than
prevented. You may know the story by now. He would
ask His Son, Jesus Christ, to take on the form of a human being, be born as a baby in a dark and crowded
stable, live a sinless life, die a sacrificial death, and then
rise from the grave triumphant. The choice of free will
would then be changed. Where once the question was,

"Shall I sin or not?" it was now, "When I sin, shall I ask to be forgiven?" Even before the first sin was committed, the perfect antidote was in place.

We don't often associate Christmas with forgiveness—joy, peace, and comfort perhaps. But when you think about it, the primary theme of the Nativity is forgiveness. Jesus came to earth that we might receive the Father's forgiveness and live as we were created to live. The manger is about hope—God's plan restored.

Unto Us a Child
Is Born

God sent the little Christ child
So man might understand
That a little child shall lead them
To that unknown Promised Land.
For God in His great wisdom
Knew that men would rise to power
And forget His holy precepts
In their great triumphal hour. . .
He knew that they would question
And doubt the holy birth
And turn their time and talents
To the pleasures of this earth. . .

But every new discovery
Is an open avenue
To more and greater mysteries,
And man's search is never through. . .
And man can never fathom
The mysteries of the Lord
Or understand His promise
Of a heavenly reward. . .
And no one but a little child
With simple faith and love
Can lead man's straying footsteps
To higher realms above.

~ H S R

So Precious to Him

[God] chose us in him before the creation of the world to be holy and blameless in his sight. In love he predestined us for adoption to sonship through Jesus Christ, in accordance with his pleasure and will.

EPHESIANS 1:4–5 NIV

Have you ever wondered why Almighty God would choose to send His Son to earth in the body of a helpless infant? Why not a wise philosopher or a conquering hero? And how did He choose the woman who would be Jesus' mother? It would have seemed sensible to entrust the Christ child—the one the entire plan was depending on—to a mature woman with a fair amount of resources and status rather than a poor peasant girl still in her teens.

But God knew what He was doing. Mary was chosen because her heart was pure. She could be trusted to obey without question, and she was a virgin, fit to receive the holy child of God. Jesus was born as a baby so that He could demonstrate that He was a fitting sacrifice, having fulfilled the law with His sinless life. Though we are incapable of understanding God's thoughts or reasoning, He has chosen to share these few explanations with us in His Word.

As you approach Christmas this year, think about the intricacy and perfection of God's plan to redeem you. He left nothing to chance. Each step was orchestrated and played out on the world stage in dramatic detail. The prophecies of old were fulfilled, the precepts of the law were observed, and the extremities of man's heart were accounted for.

It should make you feel very loved to know the Creator of the universe went to such lengths to redeem you. *Why* you are so precious to Him—yet another mystery. But *that* you are precious has been stated and proven by God Himself. Remember that this Christmas, dear friend.

The Presence of Jesus

Jesus came into this world one glorious Christmas eve.
He came to live right here on earth to help us to believe.
For God up in His heaven knew His children all would feel
That if Jesus lived among them they would know that He was real
And not a far-off stranger who dwelt up in the sky
And knew neither joys nor sorrows that make us laugh and cry.
And so He walked among us and taught us how to love
And promised us that someday we would dwell with Him above.
And while we cannot see Him as they did, face-to-face,
We know that He is everywhere, not in some far-off place.

~ H S R

The Great Christmas Miracle

*The Word became flesh and
made his dwelling among us.*

JOHN 1:14 NIV

The incarnation of Christ—God coming to earth as a human being, taking the form of an infant—is much more than amazing; it really can't be adequately described. We are left to try to work it out in our minds with analogies.

Suppose you are walking around your yard and you come upon an anthill. You bend down and look carefully at the little creatures scurrying around, completely unaware of your presence. Perhaps you pick up a stick and poke the hill, but even then the ants notice only the disruption in their path—not the hand that is extended above. You figure it might be time for another tactic, so you yell out, "Hey, you ants. Look up! Can you see me? Can you hear me? I'm talking to you!" But nothing changes. The ants go right on about their business.

When God created man, He knew it would be tough to communicate one-on-one with His created ones. He is, after all, so big, and we are so small. He placed in man a spirit, a divine microchip so that we could see and hear Him. But sin ruined the chip and cut us off from Him. That left Him with just one solution—to reestablish communication, He had to become one of us. Imagine that! Suppose you were asked to become an ant in order to communicate with them?

Think about that as you celebrate Christmas, dear friend. Consider what God did, what lengths He was willing to go to in order to get us to see Him, to hear Him. It's the greatest Christmas miracle of all.

This Is the Savior
of the World

Some regard the Christmas story as something
     beautiful to hear,
A lovely Christmas custom that we celebrate each year.
But it's more than just a story told to make
     our hearts rejoice;
It's our Father up in heaven speaking through
     the Christ child's voice,
Telling us of heavenly kingdoms that He has
     prepared above
For those who put their trust in His mercy and His love.
And only through the Christ child can man be born again,
For God sent the baby Jesus as the Savior of all men.

~ H S R

The Power of the Crèche

*John [the Baptist] gave this testimony: "I saw
the Spirit come down from heaven as a dove. . . .
I have seen and I testify that this is God's Chosen One."*

JOHN 1:32, 34 NIV

Jesus and His disciples were walking through the
countryside of Caesarea one day. As they rested for a
few minutes, Jesus asked them, "Who do people say that
I am?" Though they had spent most of every waking moment together, Jesus wasn't convinced that they knew
for a certainty who He really was. Peter, never reluctant
to speak up, answered, "You are the Christ, the Son of
the living God." Jesus was obviously pleased. They knew
Him. Jesus told Peter he was blessed because of the
revelation of who He is and what He is doing here. Jesus
even said that Peter's words would be the rock on which
the body of believers from all over the earth would be
established. To them He would deliver the keys to the
kingdom of heaven. (See Matthew 16:13–20.)

Do you know who Jesus really is? As you set your
nativity out this Christmas season, hold the crèche in
your hand for a moment. Look carefully at the tiny infant

lying there. Do you see who He really is? Have you received the understanding Peter had, the insight for which Jesus blessed him? This baby—tiny and helpless though He seems—is the Son of the living God. Establishing that truth in your heart is the greatest gift you will ever receive—this Christmas or any Christmas. It places in your hand the keys to the kingdom of heaven, opening to you all the glorious benefits of sonship, including eternal life. Imagine that!

Tie a little bow around the crèche with the Christ child as a reminder, if you like. Every time you walk past, you'll appreciate your gift even more.

Gloria in Excelsis Deo

A star in the sky, an angel's voice
Telling the world—Rejoice! Rejoice!
But that was centuries and centuries ago,
And we ask today was it really so?
Was the Christ child born in a manger-bed
Without a pillow to rest His head?
Did He walk on earth and live and die
And return to God to dwell on high?

We were not there to hear or see,
But our hopes and dreams of eternity
Are centered around that holy story
When God sent us His Son in glory—
And life on earth has not been the same,
Regardless of what the skeptics claim,
For no event ever left behind
A transformation of this kind. . .

So question and search and doubt, if you will,
But the story of Christmas is living still. . .
And though man may conquer the earth and the sea,
He cannot conquer eternity. . .
And with all his triumph man is but a clod
Until he comes to rest with God.

~ H S R

Treasure These Things in Your Heart

His mother treasured all these things
in her heart. And Jesus grew in wisdom
and stature, and in favor with God and man.

LUKE 2:51–52 NIV

Opinions differ about Christmas. For some it is the holiday of holidays, the crowning event of the year. For others, it is little more than a bother with all its shopping and baking and wrapping. Most of us fall somewhere in the middle. Truly understanding what happened that day in Bethlehem, however, changes everything for everyone, dear friend. Rather than just a period of gaiety and good cheer, Christmas can be seen for what it truly is, the pivotal point in history, the most amazing act of kindness and sacrifice ever. God became one of us in order to bring us back to Himself. This celebration embraces more than the month of December; it literally touches every corner of our lives, every day of the year. It can't even be contained in the fullness of history, but carries us deftly into the realm of eternal life.

In light of that, dear friend, do what you can to make this your best Christmas ever, the year that you come to understand the presence of God in your life and the implications of His remarkable love for you. Unwrap your gifts, partake of the ham and the turkey, festoon your home with lights. But don't leave God's gift unopened. Wait until you have a quiet moment; then lift your eyes to His. Thank Him for sending Jesus, in the form of a child. Thank Him for making a way for you, placing a light in the darkness, reconciling you to your heavenly Father.

Then you can truly experience Christmas every day of the year.

What Christmas Means to Me

Christmas to me is a gift from above,
A gift of salvation born of God's love.
For far beyond what my mind comprehends,
My eternal future completely depends
On that first Christmas night centuries ago
When God sent His Son to the earth below.
For if the Christ child had not been born,
There would be no rejoicing on Easter morn.
For only because Christ was born and died
And hung on a cross to be crucified
Can worldly sinners like you and me
Be fit to live in eternity.
So Christmas is more than getting and giving;
It's the why and wherefore of infinite living.
It's the positive proof for doubting God never,
For in His kingdom, life is forever.
And this is the reason that on Christmas Day
I can only kneel and prayerfully say,
"Thank You, God, for sending Your Son
So that when my work on earth is done,
I can look at last on Your holy face,
Knowing You saved me alone by Your grace."

~ H S R

Christmas in My Heart

Dear Father, I receive your gift so kindly given—the gift of Your Son, born of a virgin, crucified, dead, buried, and risen from the grave—for me. In return I give You my love and devotion, and I will carry Christmas in my heart all year long. Amen.

About
Helen Steiner Rice

Born in 1900 in Ohio, Helen Steiner Rice began writing at an early age. In 1918 Helen took a job at a public utilities company, eventually becoming one of the first female advertising managers and public speakers in the country. At age twenty-nine, she married banker Franklin Rice, who committed suicide in 1932, never having recovered mentally and financially from losses incurred during the Great Depression.

Following her husband's death, Helen used her gift of verse to encourage others. Her talents came to the attention of the nation when her greeting card poem "The Priceless Gift of Christmas" was read on *The Lawrence Welk Show*. Soon a series of poetry books, a source of inspiration to people worldwide, followed. Helen died in 1981, leaving a foundation that offers assistance to the needy and elderly.

SCRIPTURE INDEX

Notes

_____
_____
_____
_____
_____
_____
_____
_____
_____
_____
_____
_____
_____
_____
_____
_____
_____
_____

Notes

Notes

_____

_____

_____

_____

_____

_____

_____

_____

_____

_____

_____

_____

_____

_____

_____

_____

_____

Notes

Notes

